GALAXY OF SUPERSTARS

98°	Faith Hill
Ben Affleck	Lauryn Hill
Jennifer Aniston	Jennifer Lopez
Backstreet Boys	Ricky Martin
Brandy	Ewan McGregor
Garth Brooks	Mike Myers
Mariah Carey	'N Sync
Matt Damon	Gwyneth Paltrow
Cameron Diaz	LeAnn Rimes
Leonardo DiCaprio	Adam Sandler
Céline Dion	Will Smith
Sarah Michelle Gellar	Britney Spears
Tom Hanks	Spice Girls
Hanson	Jonathan Taylor Thomas
Jennifer Love Hewitt	Venus Williams

CHELSEA HOUSE PUBLISHERS

GALAXY OF SUPERSTARS

Gwyneth Paltrow

Anne E. Hill

CHELSEA HOUSE PUBLISHERS
Philadelphia

Frontis: Aside from her distinguished acting abilities, Gwyneth Paltrow is often associated with her particularly keen sense of fashion.

CHELSEA HOUSE PUBLISHERS

Editor in Chief: Sally Cheney
Associate Editor in Chief: Kim Shinners
Production Manager: Pamela Loos
Art Director: Sara Davis

Produced by
21st Century Publishing and Communications, Inc.
New York, New York
http://www.21cpc.com

The Chelsea House World Wide Web address is
http://www.chelseahouse.com

First Printing

1 3 5 7 9 8 6 4 2

Library of Congress Cataloging-in-Publication Data

Hill, Anne E., 1974–
    Gwyneth Paltrow / Anne E. Hill.
        p. cm. – (Galaxy of superstars)
    Includes bibliographical references and index.
    Summary: A biography of the actress who won an Academy Award for
her performance in the movie "Shakespeare in Love."
ISBN 0-7910-6463-8 (alk. paper)
1. Paltrow, Gwyneth—Juvenile literature 2. Motion picture actors and
actresses—United States—Biography—Juvenile literature. [1. Paltrow,
Gwyneth. 2. Actors and actresses. 3. Women—Biography.] I. Title. II. Series.

PN2287.P225 H55 2001
791.43'028'092—dc21
[B]   2001032492

Dedication: For Sandy, my fellow die-hard Gwyneth fan. To Maksel and George, for putting up with us! And for Burchell, the nonbeliever.

Acknowledgments: Thanks mom, for taking me to see Gwyneth in action. I'll never forget our wonderful weekend with the stars!

Contents

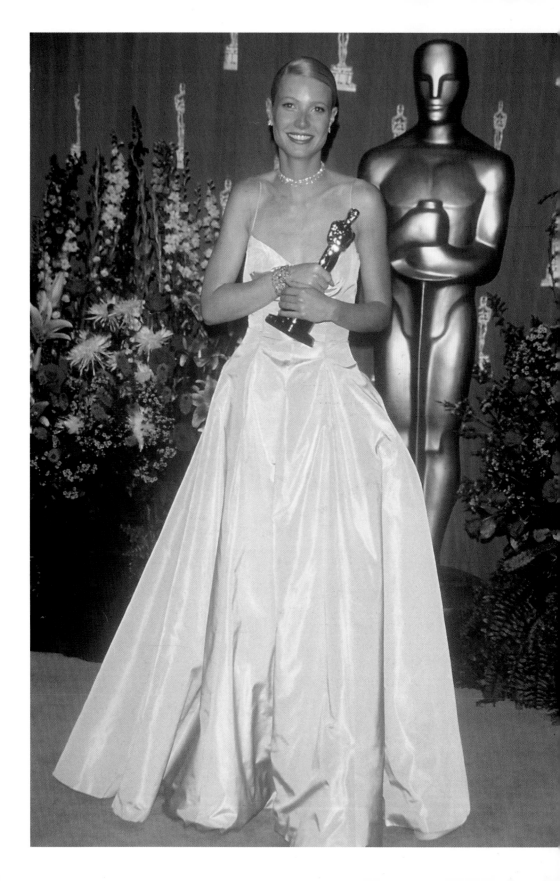

1

THE NIGHT THAT CHANGED HER LIFE

Gwyneth Paltrow was glad she had her father's arm for support as she stepped out onto the long red carpet in front of the Dorothy Chandler Pavilion in downtown Los Angeles on March 21, 1999. As a nominee for Best Actress at this Academy Awards ceremony, she was filled with anticipation. But she looked every bit the picture of cool sophistication as she greeted the media and waved to the hundreds of fans in the spectators' stands.

In her cotton candy pink gown, Gwyneth also looked the picture of Hollywood beauty. Her natural glow of excitement was enhanced by the beautiful, gleaming diamonds on loan from jewelry designer Harry Winston. Her blonde hair was swept up and off her face. She admitted to reporters that it had been very difficult to decide which designer dress to wear for this important night. Everyone seemed to agree that she had made the right decision. She quickly became one of the most photographed people at the awards. "It's flattering but a bit embarrassing. I don't want to take away attention from the other nominees. It was hard deciding what to wear, but this dress was just so pretty, and I feel good in it," she said.

On the evening of March 21, 1999, Gwyneth Paltrow walked down the red carpet outside of the Dorothy Chandler Pavilion in Los Angeles on her way to an Academy Award for Best Actress. She won the Oscar for her role in *Shakespeare in Love*.

To the media, perhaps even more important than the subject of her gown, was Gwyneth's chance of winning the Best Actress award. She faced stiff competition from actress Cate Blanchett who was nominated for her stunning portrayal of the titular queen in *Elizabeth.* Some critics believed Gwyneth's role as Lady Viola, the fictional muse to young playwright William Shakespeare in the critically acclaimed *Shakespeare in Love,* had not been as challenging as Cate's role, while others claimed the award rightfully belonged to Gwyneth.

She wasn't worrying about odds or favorites tonight, however. The 26-year-old actress declared that she was just thrilled to be there. Unlike many of those assembled that night, winning wouldn't necessarily fulfill one of Gwyneth's dreams. Instead she claimed:

> [Winning is] not really something I think about. Sure as a kid, you're like, 'Wow, I wonder what that would be like to be nominated or to win.' But I never did the 'thank you' thing in front of the mirror, and it's certainly not a goal. . . . It shouldn't be the focus. It shouldn't be the goal. . . . [J]ust having my parents come to the screening . . . and seeing them both cry at the end; to me, that was all I needed.

Still, Gwyneth must have been wondering what she would say if she won that night as she joined the other celebrities filing into the auditorium for the show. She had plenty of time to contemplate if she would win: at four hours and two minutes, the show turned out to be longest Academy Awards on record. Gwyneth sat with her father and mother and chatted

Gwyneth arrived at the 1999 Academy Awards on the arm of her father, producer/ director Bruce Paltrow. She was nominated for her portrayal of the fictional character Viola, Shakespeare's romantic inspiration for *Romeo and Juliet*.

with them between awards, which were given out in nearly every category before the nominees for Best Actress were read. Gwyneth cheered as costar Judi Dench won in the Best Supporting Actress category. Finally, it was time to announce Best Actress.

After her name was announced as the winner, Gwyneth looked genuinely shocked. But when she got to the podium, she seemed collected. She was poised as she began her acceptance speech. But in the middle of thanking those she loved, Gwyneth was overcome with emotion. As her proud parents watched, a sobbing Gwyneth thanked her "mommy" as well as her dad, brother, and grandparents. "I would not have been able to play this role had I not understood love of a tremendous magnitude, and for that, I thank my family," she said. Her lack of composure at the end of her speech endeared Gwyneth to fans and even to her critics who had previously dubbed her too icy and composed. She was able to laugh about it later, "Could I have been wimpier? No, I was positive I wouldn't win. . . . So I was completely unprepared. I just started crying, and I couldn't stop." She was simply stunned by the honor and all it meant. She said that when her name was announced:

> I'd never had such a keen sense of surreality in my life. I had that feeling, like, when you have a dream and you're trying to run but you can't? I thought, I'm not going to be able to make my legs go up the stairs. I don't even remember what I said. And then it was over, and thank God, Steven Spielberg was in the wings, because he's a real close family friend, and I really needed somebody I knew right then.

Spielberg, who gave Gwyneth her first break when he cast the teen as Wendy in *Hook*, was the first of many to congratulate Gwyneth that night. Many others were eager to give their best wishes. Her parents and grandparents, including her beloved Grandpa "Buster" Paltrow, escorted Gwyneth to the after-parties. "She was just so wonderful tonight," her mother, actress Blythe Danner, said. "I think that she can't believe that at 26 she has won this honor."

It was true, Gwyneth couldn't believe she had won — she certainly never expected to win. Just weeks before the awards, she had bet two talent agents at Creative Artists Agency each $1,000 that she wouldn't win the award. She paid them off in the lobby, in cash, just after her win. It was one loss she didn't mind.

The rest of the night was unlike anything Gwyneth had ever experienced. "The whole thing is like a dream," she later admitted. But it was a good dream, the perfect end to a hard year for the actress. There had been personal struggles, after both her father and grandfather had been diagnosed with cancer, in addition to the challenge of making *Shakespeare in Love* on location in England. "I've never worked so hard on anything in my life," Gwyneth admitted. "I was so spent to the bone every day. I was using everything that I had, not only because I was dealing with research of the period, but also I had to keep everything straight about whether I was a boy or girl."

Shakespeare in Love tells the fictitious story of young William Shakespeare, a struggling but gifted playwright, who has temporarily lost his inspiration and cannot write a play for which he has already received partial payment. The comedy he has been asked to write, *Romeo and Ethel, the Pirate's Daughter*, turns into the tragic romance of *Romeo and Juliet*, once he meets the beautiful and wealthy Lady Viola, played by Gwyneth. But what Will doesn't know about his new love is that not only is she engaged to be married, she is also impersonating a man so she can act a part in his play. (In the late 16th and early 17th centuries, women were not allowed to act in plays. Female roles were usually played by young boys whose voices had not changed.) When Will discovers Viola's own love for the theater, it only increases his passion for her. They fall in love despite the fact that they know it can't end happily.

The love story was the first on many critics' lists for the best films of the year. The movie received a total of seven Academy Awards, including Best Picture, beating out Steven Spielberg's World War II drama, *Saving Private Ryan.*

The cast and crew of *Shakespeare* worked many long hours to bring the story to life. Gwyneth believed the role was as challenging physically as it was mentally. The costumes were heavy, and she had to wear a fake mustache and learn to move like a man, even though she is not sure she ever convinced anyone she wasn't really a woman. Luckily, then boyfriend Ben Affleck was there to joke with her when the cameras weren't rolling. He took a small role in the film and traveled to England to be close to Gwyneth.

There was also the task of training for the role in terms of accent and manner. Fortunately, not only was Gwyneth no stranger to Shakespeare, but she had grown up watching her mother perform. Despite these advantages and her good ear for accents, Gwyneth still opted to work with a dialect coach to perfect her British accent. The results were worth the extra effort. "Her ability to hit the accent is extraordinary," said her costar Joseph Fiennes, the English actor who played Shakespeare. As a further testament to Gwyneth's dedication she worked with an acting coach from the Royal Shakespeare Company on text, voice, and articulation.

By the time filming wrapped, Gwyneth was

exhilarated and exhausted. She had a good feeling about *Shakespeare in Love*, but she didn't know it would change her life. Ironically, the movie had been developed for Julia Roberts and Daniel Day-Lewis, and Gwyneth had initially passed on it as well. She thought she did not have the energy at the time to handle such a large and daunting role.

She proved more than capable. In addition to taking home the Oscar, Gwyneth also won a Golden Globe for Best Actress in a Drama and a Screen Actors Guild award. Gwyneth had finally stepped out of the shadow of her famous mother, Blythe Danner, and her ex-fiancé, Brad Pitt.

Ever since she had been a little girl, she wanted to act, and now she had reached her goal.

Gwyneth had to work on her British accent for her award-winning role in *Shakespeare in Love*. In addition to Gwyneth's winning for Best Actress, the film also won the Academy Award for Best Picture.

2

A PRIVILEGED BEGINNING

It's no surprise that Gwyneth aspired to be an actress. After all, she is the daughter of Tony Award-winning actress Blythe Danner and producer/director Bruce Paltrow. Gwyneth Kate Paltrow was born on September 28, 1972, in Los Angeles, California. Blythe and Bruce named their first-born child after a Pennsylvania philanthropist who influenced Danner when she was a child growing up outside Philadelphia in the wealthy Main Line area. Three years after Gwyneth was born, her brother Jake completed the family.

The Paltrows lived in a beach house near Malibu, California, surrounded by other up-and-coming entertainers, including Steven Spielberg, whom Gwyneth now lovingly calls "Uncle Morty." While the Paltrows enjoyed their close-knit social circle, there were doubts if Blythe and Bruce's mixed-faith marriage would last. Willowy, blonde Danner was raised as Christian, while Bruce Paltrow is Jewish. Today, Gwyneth embraces both religions. "I consider myself half-and-half," she said. "The people who don't know me get the WASP [white, Anglo-Saxon Protestant]. And the people who

Gwyneth Kate Paltrow was born in Los Angeles to actress Blythe Danner and producer/director Bruce Paltrow. Gwyneth's family lived in a beach house near Malibu, California, close to many famous Hollywood stars.

know me get the Jew." The Paltrows did stay together, and Gwyneth holds her parents' long-lasting marriage as a model and inspiration. She claims family is the most important thing to her and says that after she is married and has children, they will take priority over her career.

During the summer, the Paltrow family would migrate east to Williamstown, Massachusetts, in the Berkshire Mountains, where Danner would take the stage at the seasonal Williamstown Theater Festival. Gwyneth was barely out of diapers in 1974, when her mother was rehearsing for a production of Anton Chekhov's *The Seagull.* Little Gwyneth shocked her mother by reciting Danner's speech in the play. "She didn't have anything on except her golden curls," recalled Danner. "She could barely talk, yet she knew the whole speech better than I did. . . . That was the beginning. We should have known then, I guess."

It didn't take long for Gwyneth to get bitten by the acting bug. Between her mother's rehearsals and performances and accompanying her father as he made the rounds of Hollywood production studios, the youngster was well exposed to the thrill of the entertainment world.

When she was five years old, Danner allowed Gwyneth to have a walk-on role in a play at the Williamstown Theater Festival. Soon, Gwyneth was taking other small roles and relishing the spotlight. At one cabaret act that the Williamstown actors often stage after the regular show, six-year-old Gwyneth sang a duet, "Anything You Can Do, I Can Do Better" with another future actor, Christian Slater. Danner recalled, "[D]uring the applause, I saw this look in her eye, and I said to my husband,

'Oh, she's discovered it. Now she knows the thrill.'" One of Gwyneth's fondest memories was when she was seven years old and spent the summer of 1979 in Beaufort, South Carolina, watching her mother film *The Great Santini* with Robert Duvall.

Danner and Paltrow didn't push their daughter into show business. Instead, Gwyneth spent her early years at an alternative school called St. Augustine by the Sea in Santa Monica. "She's so similar to how she was as a child," Gwyneth's kindergarten friend Mary Wigmore told *Vanity Fair* magazine. "She was always

Gwyneth's parents encouraged their daughter's flair for acting but did not push her into show business. She first performed at the Williamstown Theater Festival when she was five years old.

really funny and bright and she always loved the details." Gwyneth still managed to get into her fair share of trouble as a kid. "We'd throw stuffed animals into the chimney next door, and play Dingdong Ditch—ring someone's doorbell and run away," Wigmore recalls.

Soon, however, Gwyneth was forced to leave behind the friends she made in Southern California for New York City. Blythe and Bruce decided the move to Manhattan's Upper East Side was best for their family. "It was very important to my mother that we be raised for the latter part [of our childhoods] in [New York]," Gwyneth explained. "I think she found so many aspects of L.A. superficial. There's so much culture in New York, the museums and the theater. Just walking down the street . . . you're exposed to everything."

Eleven-year-old Gwyneth was enrolled at the prestigious, all-girls Spence School. The academically demanding institution's students studied law and physics in seventh grade. "I could barely do anything. Except express myself," she remembered. While Gwyneth claims she struggled to fit in at Spence, her friend Julia Cuddihy called her a leader who set fashion trends with her long hair, Levi's jeans, cowboy boots, and make-up-free face. Gwyneth says she was never an official part of the "cool group" at school, instead drifting in and out of favor with the in-crowd. Gwyneth claims to have been the shortest girl in her class and didn't develop until her mid-teens (she is now 5' 9"). But she still found her niche as a member of the a cappella singing group Triple Trio. Her vocal talent landed her solos and she led the group in her favorite song at the time, Billy Joel's

"Uptown Girl." In fact, Gwyneth's talent as a singer led many to believe that she would become a singer rather than an actress.

Instead, Gwyneth's sights were set on an acting career. She became even more determined at age 13 after watching her mother play the role of Blanche DuBois in Tennessee Williams's classic *A Streetcar Named Desire*. She recalled:

> I had just returned from camp in Burlington, Vermont. I had never read the play or seen a rehearsal. I went to the opening night and sat with my father, and my mom was too much. I just saw her come completely apart in front of me. It was the most profound experience. It was the most powerful, moving thing I'd ever seen in my entire life. She was so extraordinary, so gifted. Afterward, when I went backstage in her dressing room, all I could do was weep. I held on to her and I cried and cried and cried.

Suddenly, Gwyneth didn't want to do anything other than act. Her summers in Williamstown became more focused on honing her skills, while back at home she starred in school productions, playing Titania, Queen of the Fairies, in Shakespeare's *A Midsummer Night's Dream*. "It was really an exceptional way to grow up, because I was both in the realm of the acceptable world and also a carnie kid or a gypsy," Gwyneth has said of her childhood. "On one hand, I had this great East Coast private-girls-school education. On the other, I would go to rehearsals with my mother and sit barefoot and cross-legged watching her work."

Watching her mother's performances inspired Gwyneth. Blythe successfully managed both career and family. In fact, Gwyneth has always admired her mother's ability to turn down roles even more than her ability to shine in them. "It makes me feel loved and important because a lot of people wanted her to work, but I never felt like it was a sacrifice for her." But Danner and Paltrow were strict with both Gwyneth and Jake, who had made mention of his interest in directing, like his father. The two were urged to get an education and not rush into show business.

So instead of spending the spring of her sophomore year of high school auditioning and performing, Gwyneth took part in an exchange program in Spain. Members of her host family liked to stay out late and party. Their ways caught on with 15-year-old Gwyneth. When she returned home to New York, she had entered a rebellious phase. She snuck out of her parent's house and frequented New York night-spots, only to end up being grounded the next morning.

But staying out late at night wasn't teenage Gwyneth's only bad habit. She began slipping in her school work as well, and her grades reflected that. While she was naturally bright, Gwyneth was casual in her approach toward studying and attending classes. She wasn't able to get into any of the top colleges due to her mediocre college board scores. She was rejected by both Vassar College and Williams College (home of the Williamstown Theater Festival).

Family friend and University of California at Santa Barbara (UCSB) alumnus, Michael

Gwyneth admires her mother's ability to have both a career and a family. Even though she is a successful actress, Blythe Danner always put her family first.

Douglas, intervened on Gwyneth's behalf, helping her get accepted into the large, beachside university. After she graduated from Spence in the spring of 1990, Gwyneth took a semester off, then packed her bags and headed to college in California. While she intended to study art history when she arrived in Santa Barbara in the winter of 1991, Gwyneth was also excited that Los Angeles was just an hour to the south. She could make it to auditions and still go to class.

She was soon missing classes in favor of driving into L.A. It didn't take long for Gwyneth to realize that college wasn't for her. "It was such an inappropriate place for me to be. I just felt something bigger out there waiting," Gwyneth remembered. "I didn't know what it was. I didn't know if it had something to do with acting or love or, as it turned out, both of these things." Gwyneth confessed her feelings to both of her parents, who urged her to stay in school. Gwyneth didn't want to disappoint her parents, but she also wanted to convince them that college wasn't the place for her.

She did just that in the summer of 1991, after completing one semester at UCSB. Gwyneth returned to Willamstown to star in a production of *Picnic* with her mother. Following a dress rehearsal for the play, Bruce Paltrow came backstage and told 18-year-old Gwyneth how impressed he was with her performance and that he didn't think she should return to school. "It's probably the one moment in my life that was truly one of the most amazing things and at the same time was really a definitive thing." Gwyneth also got rave reviews for the role.

With her parents' support, Gwyneth did not return to college. Instead, she prepared to take a bold and uncertain step. Gwyneth was ready to see if she could become a professional actress.

3

HOLLYWOOD BECKONS

With two prominent and wealthy parents, Gwyneth's transition from student to actress could have been an easy one. Her parents could both pay her way and help get her parts. However, the Paltrows made it clear early on that they were not going to support their daughter financially, nor were they going to pull any strings to get her roles. Instead, Gwyneth moved into a small Hollywood apartment and got a job as a waitress at the trendy upscale DC3, located near the Santa Monica airport. Gwyneth didn't mind struggling to make ends meet. She spent what little money she made on necessities and then got accustomed to the L.A. bar and club scene.

Her parents' friends had also become Gwyneth's, including the famous director Steven Spielberg. Late in the summer of 1991, Spielberg accompanied Gwyneth and Bruce to see the thriller film *Silence of the Lambs*. Spielberg was in the middle of trying to cast the role of a young Wendy in his film *Hook*, a continuation of the classic *Peter Pan*. While they were waiting in line for tickets to see *Silence*, Spielberg asked Gwyneth if she would take a small role. Gwyneth was thrilled.

Despite her famous parents, Gwyneth earned her own way on to the Hollywood scene, supporting herself as a waitress until she began to land movie roles. She quickly became a rising star in the movie industry.

Before she knew it, she had an agent in addition to her first film role. Rick Kurtzman of the Creative Artists Agency remembers that, even though Gwyneth was still a teenager, "there was also something very adult about her." Kurtzman didn't take Paltrow on because of her well-known family. "It wasn't about her mother. It was about committing myself to give someone else my time and energy. Unless you feel it passionately, you can't do it."

With Kurtzman's help, Gwyneth was soon landing more work. In 1991, in addition to appearing in *Hook*, Gwyneth made the film *Shout* with John Travolta. While neither film was a critical or financial success, Paltrow wasn't discouraged. She turned her attention to television work, starring in the 1992 mini-series *Cruel Doubt*. Ironically, her real-life mom was later cast as her mother in the film. This time, it was Gwyneth who had helped her mother get work. Danner explains: "She got the part first, and I guess they thought I looked right as her mother."

While she was enjoying working, and even attaining some success, there were many roles that Gwyneth didn't get. After five callbacks for Woody Allen's 1992 film *Husbands and Wives*, Gwyneth lost the part to not one but two actresses. Her friend Emily Lloyd was originally cast in the role, but dropped out, only to be replaced by Juliette Lewis. "I cried," Gwyneth admits. It wasn't the only time she faced rejection. "It was between me and Julia Ormond for *Legends of the Fall*. And there was Moira Kelly, Samantha Mathis, Natasha Gregson Wagner, Lara Flynn Boyle . . . " she says of the long list of talented competitors she faced at each and every audition.

Gwyneth was the director and casting agents' choice, however, for the 1993 drama *Flesh and Bone.* "She had tons of spontaneity and raw nerve," recalled writer and director Steve Kloves. "You could feel the confidence." Gwyneth's confidence never wavered, even when costarring opposite the likes of Dennis Quaid, Meg Ryan, and James Caan. She played Ginnie, a thief and con artist who steals jewelry off corpses in west Texas.

While the film was a box office disappointment and didn't get great reviews, Gwyneth was singled out for her performance. Mike Clark, from *USA Today* wrote: "Gwyneth Paltrow might have gotten a supporting Oscar nomination had the film not flopped." Even notoriously tough film critic Roger Ebert of the *Chicago Sun-Times* was impressed with Gwyneth. He wrote: "The real-eye opener . . . is Gwyneth Paltrow, who more than holds her own playing opposite three established stars. Her performance as the sexy, cynical Ginnie is fresh and unaffected, and it doesn't take long for us to get into the character's head to understand her motives and crushed dreams."

Paltrow was understandably excited by the reviews. She shared her happiness with her parents as well as new boyfriend, actor Robert Sean Leonard. Soon, it was back to work, costarring in another television movie— *Deadly Relations,* with Robert Urich, and the big-feature thriller *Malice,* starring Alec Baldwin, Nicole Kidman, and Bill Pullman. Gwyneth was hoping for that one film that would help her rise above her peers and earn her acclaim as an actress. When she heard she was in the running to take the lead in the remake of *Sabrina,* starring Harrison Ford,

Gwyneth thought it might be her big break. Ultimately, the role again went to Julia Ormond.

Still, Gwyneth was being noticed. She made *Rolling Stone* magazine's list of hot breakout stars in 1994, joining the music group Green Day and actor Leonardo DiCaprio. Also in 1994, Gwyneth starred in *Mrs. Parker and the Vicious Circle* with Jennifer Jason Leigh and Matthew Broderick. "I'll never forget that first table read," recalls Leigh. "Maybe she was 20. A real girl's girl when she arrived. Then this other person came out of her with such grace and confidence. The entire cast fell in love with her right then."

Her fellow cast members weren't the only ones falling for Gwyneth. Some casting agents were also clamoring for her attention. She was cast in three films that were released back-to-back in 1995: two dramas and a thriller. The idea that she was a sought-after actress was both relieving and reassuring to Gwyneth. She had decided that if she hadn't achieved some success by the time her friends had graduated from college, she had made the wrong decision in dropping out of school.

But there was no denying that Gwyneth's career was taking off. She traveled to France to film her first 1995 release, *Jefferson in Paris*, a film about Thomas Jefferson's years as a U.S. ambassador in France. Gwyneth played the widowed Jefferson's oldest daughter, Patsy. It was the first of many period pieces Gwyneth would star in over the years, but not one of her most memorable. Even she admitted that the film wasn't very good. However, she was glad that she had learned French, which she had always wanted to speak.

Less than 48 hours after wrapping up

Jefferson in Paris, Gwyneth went to Williamstown, Massachusetts, where she began rehearsals for the play *The Seagull*. The two-week engagement during the summer was exhausting but exhilarating for the actress. She only had a week off after the show to relax and prepare for her next shoot—*Moonlight and Valentino*—in Toronto, Canada. Paltrow was excited to work with the other women in the film, Elizabeth Perkins, Whoopi Goldberg, and

In 1996, Gwyneth starred in the film adaptation of Jane Austen's novel *Emma*. It would prove to be one of her most successful period pieces.

Kathleen Turner. It was their participation in the film that had convinced Gwyneth to make another film so soon after *Jefferson in Paris.*

She explained to *Premiere* magazine what drives her:

> In one way, you can't believe that you're being offered movies, and you just want to work. Another part of it was a real desire to learn, to learn as much as I could. And another part is distraction: 'I don't know who I am, and I'm restless and I'm bored, and I don't know what I want.' You just work, as a distraction and as a lesson. I think it's good to work really hard when you're young. I think the more you work, the better.

Gwyneth was putting her words into action in *Moonlight and Valentino,* taking on the role of a New York University film student named Lucy who is called home after the unexpected death of her brother-in-law. Gwyneth identified with the character's quest to find out who she is, her insecurities, and her tendency to chain smoke (Gwyneth had picked up the habit as a teenager but quit after the death of her grandfather). She got great reviews for the role. Critics claimed that she stole the show away from her better-known costars. One reviewer wrote: "Best of all is Paltrow, who, on the heels of *Flesh and Bone* and *Jefferson in Paris*, is fast proving she can do anything. Her Lucy is the film's most sympathetic character, a pretty student whose tarted-up exterior belies a kind heart and troubled soul."

While Gwyneth was filming *Moonlight and Valentino*, she received a phone call from Harvey Weinstein of the independent Miramax

Studios. Weinstein wanted Gwyneth to work at Miramax, and Gwyneth wasn't sure how to respond. However, Weinstein began sending her scripts, and before long, he and Gwyneth had decided that she would star in an adaptation of Jane Austen's classic novel *Emma*.

Before filming for *Emma* began, though, Gwyneth had another movie in the works, her third of 1995, and the one that would change her life.

4

GWYNETH IN LOVE

When Gwyneth walked onto the set of *Seven*, she was thrilled to be working with Academy Award nominee Morgan Freeman and rising star Brad Pitt. She had actually met Pitt, *People* magazine's "Sexiest Man Alive," some seven months earlier. She even admitted to a friend that she had a crush on the handsome actor. However, it wasn't until the two got to know one another on the set of *Seven* that their romance began.

Even though the subject of the film had nothing to do with romance, it didn't take long for Brad and Gwyneth to become an item on the set. Pitt had actually suggested that Gwyneth play the role of his wife, Tracy. He had remembered her audition for *Legends of the Fall* and was impressed by her skills. "The Tracy character was so important, because it's the only sunshine we have in the film," Pitt explained. "We needed someone who could take those little seconds she gets and fill them with soul, and that's what I'd always seen in her performances—soul. She took a fantastic part and made it better."

For their first date, Pitt took Gwyneth to an intimate Italian restaurant where no one noticed them. That was

Gwyneth met actor Brad Pitt on the set of *Seven* in 1995, and they quickly became the hottest item in Hollywood. Even though they announced an engagement, the couple split suddenly in the summer of 1997.

practically the only time the couple wasn't photographed, questioned, or followed in public. It seemed an unlikely match—22-year-old Gwyneth came from a prominent upper-class New York City background, while 31-year-old Pitt was a middle-class, blue-collar boy from the Midwest. But after seeing them together, few could deny that they were in love. The couple's pictures appeared on the cover of magazines, in newspapers, and on entertainment television shows even before *Seven* premiered.

Unfortunately, their photos also appeared online—without the couple's knowledge or permission. In May 1995, Gwyneth and Pitt took a vacation to the Caribbean island of St. Bart's. While they were lounging on the private balcony of their secluded hotel, a photographer took revealing pictures. The photos first appeared in a British newspaper and then on the popular Internet service provider America Online. The couple had learned the hard way that they were forever going to be in the public eye. Gwyneth later said: "I'm not someone who carries bitter memories, but any reasonable person can see that there were no limits to how far the paparazzi would go to maintain a state of near-constant surveillance on us. You begin to develop a siege mentality."

As working actors, Brad and Gwyneth were often separated while working on different film locations. Gwyneth had decided that even though the separation was hard, she wanted to keep working. She refused to be seen as famous for being Brad Pitt's girlfriend. Before *Seven* even wrapped, she started filming *Hard Eight*, in which she played a prostitute. She followed the role in *Hard Eight* with that of

David Schwimmer's character's love interest in the flop *The Pallbearer*. Gwyneth wasn't particularly interested in making the comedy about a high school loser who is asked to be a pallbearer at a classmate's funeral where he reunites with his high school crush (played by Gwyneth), but Miramax executives asked that she make the movie before they started *Emma*. Paltrow admitted resenting the politics of getting to star in *Emma*.

Still, she traveled to England to film *Emma* in the summer of 1995. She worked on her British accent and brought to life the character of Emma Woodhouse, one of Jane Austen's most beloved heroines. "She's a . . . very good person," Gwyneth said of the character. "She's just a little spoiled: her mother has died and she's grown up with a father who thinks she can do no wrong. What I loved about her so much is that she has faults; it's nice to see a film heroine who makes terrible mistakes and really learned from them and is very pained by them."

While even the English cast and crew were impressed with Gwyneth's English accent, it was her New York accent and dead-on Woody Allen impression that had them in stitches. She also carried a coffee mug with Brad Pitt's picture on it around the set.

However, the effect of doing so many films in a row was beginning to wear on Gwyneth. After *Emma*, she traveled to the Sundance Film Festival in Park City, Utah, to see the premiere of her brother Jake's first film. She also planned to spend time with Pitt in his newly purchased Los Angeles mansion. The two decided that after shooting two more films, *Hush* and *Great Expectations*, Gwyneth would

The success of *Emma* in 1996 marked a turning point in Gwyneth's career. She was offered many starring roles, including the part of Estella in the 1998 film adaptation of Charles Dickens's novel *Great Expectations*.

accompany Brad to the location of his next film, *Seven Years in Tibet*.

In the meantime there was the incredible reaction to her performance as Emma. Critics praised her, but even more important to Gwyneth was her family's support and their kind words. Her mother claimed she was "overwhelmed" by her daughter's performance, while Gwyneth's grandpa Buster Paltrow said that talent "runs in the family." Gwyneth admitted that it was "the first movie I've done that I've been honestly thrilled by." There was even talk that Gwyneth was a contender for an Oscar nomination, but she never was nominated for the role. However, she did win a Golden Satellite Award from the International Press Academy.

Unfortunately, Gwyneth's next performance, in the thriller *Hush* with Jessica Lange, generated anything but Oscar buzz. Gwyneth had ignored the weak script in favor of working with the respected actress. She later said:

> I've never seen *Hush*, nor will I ever. But I know how bad it is. I was there. Every day. I don't need to see it. Appalling movie. What am I gonna do, lie? I think people are entitled to know what you honestly feel about your work—the movies that you've been in or the plays that you've been in— and not to be shoved propaganda just because they'll go sit in the chair and see the movie when you don't even mean it.

Great Expectations, the last film Gwyneth made in 1996, was eventually released in 1998. In this movie, based on the Dickens novel, she played the cruel and manipulative Estella to her friend, fellow actor Ethan Hawke's Finnegan Bell. The role was challenging for Gwyneth mainly because she had a nude scene in the film. While Paltrow worried about her grandparents' and father's reactions to the scene, in the end she felt that it furthered the film and was in line with her character's personality. Ultimately, the film didn't make much of an impression on critics or audiences.

Afterward, Gwyneth was happy to have time off from filming, and she spent the end of 1996 on location in Tibet with Brad. When they returned in December, the two were engaged. After denying wedding rumors for two years, they could now announce that it was official: They were getting married. Both the Pitt and Paltrow families celebrated the engagement that Christmas.

Although released in 1998, *Great Expectations* was the last film that Gwyneth worked on in 1996 before departing for a much-needed break.

There never was a wedding, however. Pitt and Gwyneth split up in June 1997, and Pitt married actress Jennifer Aniston in July 2000.

Both actors remained silent as to what went wrong in their relationship. Just a few months earlier, Gwyneth had confided in her friend, singer Madonna, that she and Pitt were planning to have children within the next two years. Gwyneth had also been spotted wearing a large emerald-cut diamond engagement ring set in platinum. Fans were sorry to hear that what seemed like a fairy-tale romance had come to an end. Of course, no one was as affected as much as Gwyneth herself. "It really changed my life," Gwyneth admitted of the breakup in 2000.

> When we split up, something changed, permanently, in me. . . . My heart sort of broke that day, and it will never be the same. I think you have to keep yourself intact in order to have a healthy relation-ship, and I didn't. I loved every second of it, but it wasn't healthy. But I wouldn't change anything. Even the things I hate most about myself for what happened—the darkest moment of it—I wouldn't change. Because it's made me what I am.

Gwyneth's parents and friends helped her through the breakup. Gwyneth later said about the time, "My life was falling apart, and it took several months before I could put myself back together. I was lucky to have good friends who helped me a lot, but hitting rock bottom emotionally is a test of your character. You learn to not feel sorry for yourself."

5

IN THE SPOTLIGHT

Gwyneth's way of not feeling sorry for herself was through work. While much of America was talking about her breakup with Brad, Gwyneth was again concentrating on her career. Before her romantic troubles, Gwyneth had finished filming *Sliding Doors*, another film that had her working on her British accent.

In the film, Gwyneth played Helen, a career woman supporting her deadbeat boyfriend. What Helen doesn't know is that her boyfriend is spending his days cheating on her. The film explores two alternate realities: Helen catching an early subway home and finding her boyfriend in the arms of another woman; and Helen missing the train and not finding out about the other woman. While the movie follows each storyline, in the end, the two merge and become one. Gwyneth immediately loved the script for the small-budget film. "It has an edge," she said. "It doesn't pander to audience expectations or their intellectual shortcomings. If you trust the film, you will be rewarded. But you have to keep on your toes. It's so rare when you come across a script that's that funny and that smart." *Sliding Doors* proved

---

In just a few years, Gwyneth became one of the most coveted actresses in Hollywood. In 1998 she starred in five movies alone: *Great Expectations, Hush, A Perfect Murder, Shakespeare in Love,* and *Sliding Doors.*

that Gwyneth could more than carry a film—
she could play both leading roles!

The movie was also intensely personal for
Gwyneth, who was struggling with making
important choices for herself, and helped her
gain insights into her own life. After it was
released and won rave reviews at Robert
Redford's Sundance Film Festival, she said:

> I'd spent all this time working and never
> taking time to understand who I am as a
> woman and what I really want, what kind
> of choices I want to make. Things started
> to become clear, not only in work but in
> getting my priorities in order. . . . This film
> resonated for me in that way because it's
> about choices and destiny.

While Gwyneth's destiny seemed to lie in
becoming a star, she wasn't obsessed with
always being in the spotlight. She was anx-
iously looking forward to filming *Duets*, a
film her father was to direct and in which she
had a smaller, supporting role. Filming was
expected to begin in September 1997, but it
was put on hold after the end of Gwyneth's
relationship with Brad because Brad was
supposed to star opposite Gwyneth. His role
was recast a year later, filled by *Felicity* star
Scott Speedman.

Throughout most of the summer of 1997,
the Paltrow-Pitt breakup made headlines in
newspapers and magazines across the country.
Luckily, Gwyneth was able to get away from it
all. In August she accepted an offer from the
women's magazine *Marie Claire* to be a "castaway" guest editor for their January 1998
issue. Gwyneth spent three days stranded on a
deserted island near Belize with only the bare

essentials, including matches, water, rice, her journal, and her thoughts. She did a lot of soul searching during her time on the island. She wrote in her journal:

> My mind takes me in a new direction every few minutes. Out of nowhere I started crying large, hot tears. Lots of things were going through my mind. Life things, love things. For a moment, sitting by my fire, I felt lonelier than I ever had in my life. . . . I just sat there crying, embracing the feeling instead of trying to talk myself out of it. . . . And when I stopped, I felt really strong and centered and quiet. I was able to look at things with a better perspective.

The timing of the adventure couldn't have been better for Paltrow. She returned home, and was ready to start working again.

Gwyneth had decided to star with family friend Michael Douglas in *A Perfect Murder*, a remake of the Alfred Hitchcock classic *Dial M for Murder*. In the film, the much older Douglas played her wealthy husband, a businessman who has fallen on hard times. Gwyneth's character, Emily, is a millionaire in her own right, so her husband hatches an elaborate plan to have her killed and inherit her money. He hires Emily's lover to murder her.

The film was a departure for Gwyneth, who had gotten used to starring in smaller budgeted films with few famous names. She was thrilled to work with Douglas but soon learned that he was the best thing about the film. "It sounded like fun but looking back there wasn't anything to sink my teeth into," she said. Indeed, critics felt the same way. One even commented that the best thing about the film was Emily's wardrobe.

Slowly, others had become fascinated with what Gwyneth wore offscreen as well as onscreen. Luckily, Gwyneth didn't mind—in fact, she understood. "Clothes are pretty much my one vice in life," she admitted. "I love to experiment. My main ambition when it comes to fashion is to achieve some kind of classic look without going overboard and without being faddish." Dozens of designers send Gwyneth their creations and hope she'll wear some of their designs. While Gwyneth likes to wear clothes from a variety of designers, her favorites include Calvin Klein, Ralph Lauren, and Donna Karan. She also loves to reinvent her look. She changes her clothing, hairstyle, and even hair color fairly often. But she always pulls it off—and sometimes manages to start a trend. Her pink Oscar dress inspired dozens of knockoffs and helped make the color popular again. When Gwyneth cut her hair to star in *Sliding Doors,* many women brought in photos of her to their hairdressers so they could get their own hair cut the same way.

Gwyneth admits: "I may not be the most confident woman in the world, but I'm sure of my aesthetic choices—I know what I like. Maybe it's because I went to a school where I had to wear a uniform. I had two gray skirts. You had to work around that gray skirt."

Others agree that her various minimalist looks are the most influential and probably most enduring in all of Hollywood. "Gwyneth's not gaudy," says makeup artist Kevyn Aucoin. "She's one of the few people who understands good taste and feels good enough about herself not to wear so much stuff that it looks like she's compensating for shortcomings in other

Gwyneth is one of the most admired stars in Hollywood for her down-to-earth fashion sense.

areas. . . . Twenty years from now, women will still be emulating and imitating her style." In the meantime, Gwyneth is being recognized for her looks and style right now. She was named to *People* magazine's list of the 50 Most Beautiful People in 1998 and 1999.

In late 1997, Gwyneth was ready to begin another relationship. She started dating up-and-coming actor and writer Ben Affleck, who, along with his friend Matt Damon, had written and starred in the acclaimed film *Good Will Hunting.* Not long after he and Gwyneth started dating, Ben won a Golden Globe and an Oscar for cowriting the movie. Gwyneth even set up her good friend, actress Winona Ryder, with Matt Damon. The happy couples were often spotted double dating.

While the media followed them out to dinner or to Hollywood premieres and parties, Gwyneth had learned from her break up with Brad to be more guarded in what she revealed to reporters. Gwyneth and Affleck were a happy couple for nearly a year and a half before they ended their relationship in December 1998. The media continued to follow them, however, claiming they were an on-again, off-again couple. The rumors began because, even though they're not a couple, Gwyneth and Ben have remained very good friends.

She explains: "Our relationship has changed several times and brought us closer in some ways and further apart at different times. I still love Ben, and he knows it. But this doesn't mean we're going to share our lives together. We haven't figured that one out. Experience has taught me not to be any more candid than that when it comes to personal matters."

Gwyneth's high-profile romance with actor Ben Affleck in 1998 left her feeling vulnerable to media scrutiny. Even though they broke up in December 1998, Gwyneth and Ben remain close friends.

When she has free time, Gwyneth likes to spend time with Ben and her other friends, most of whom she has known since her kindergarten days in Los Angeles or her seventh grade class at the Spence School. She also loves to spend time with her close-knit family. She and younger brother Jake even drove through Spain together one summer.

But when she gets a few minutes to herself, Gwyneth relishes them. "There's nothing I love to do more than wake up around nine or ten in the morning, make myself a great café au lait and read *The New York Times*. That's my way of being peaceful and enjoying my time alone."

But 1998 and 1999 were not the years for Gwyneth to be alone. After her Oscar win, Gwyneth was at the center of a whirlwind of media scrutiny that left her feeling vulnerable and self-conscious. According to her friend Julia Cuddihy, "It was a year [1999] of extreme highs and lows." Gwyneth said, "It was a lot to deal with all at once. It was a strange period. I just felt exposed and embarrassed. I was wrestling with a lot of stuff." After the Academy Awards ceremony, 26-year-old Gwyneth came down with the flu. She was sick in bed for 10 days—the price of fame had finally gotten to her. She explained to *Movieline* magazine:

> I hate that people want so much from me and that people are always asking things from me. Whether it's 'Will you come host this luncheon at my house?' or 'Will you . . .' you know, every charity, every event, every store opening. . . . A lot of the time I feel like at the expense of my own sanity and physical well-being I do all these things for everybody. So it ends up being no good, because if I'm on every charity thing, then who cares? And if I'm at every store opening, then who cares? If I'm at everything, then everyone is sick of me.

Gwyneth even admitted that she was the subject of media overkill after *Premiere* magazine informed her that she was going to be on the cover of their "Women in Hollywood" issue. She said she's tired of seeing her face on magazine covers. But with the success of *Shakespeare in Love* and her string of awards, Gwyneth was not about to dodge the spotlight any time soon.

6

THE TALENTED
MS. PALTROW

Despite all of the buzz surrounding her, Gwyneth still managed to keep her life in perspective. Getting away to Italy helped—but she wasn't there on vacation. There, Gwyneth filmed *The Talented Mr. Ripley*, the thriller based upon the Patricia Highsmith novel, during the end of 1998 and early 1999.

The thriller tells the story of Tom Ripley, a con artist, who gets hired by the wealthy father of Dickie Greenleaf to fetch his son. Dickie's living in Italy and refuses to return home. Dickie's girlfriend Marge Sherman suspects that Tom isn't who he claims to be but doesn't reveal her suspicions until it's too late. Tom manages to get away not only with murdering Dickie, but also in assuming the young man's identity.

Paltrow originally had reservations about playing Marge. She didn't think the part was very substantial and she had learned after making *A Perfect Murder* that she needed meatier roles. Fortunately, director Anthony Minghella wanted her for the part so much that he had the script reworked to develop the character.

Gwyneth took the part, and nearly a year later, on

In 1999, Gwyneth costarred with Matt Damon and Jude Law in *The Talented Mr. Ripley*.

Christmas Day 1999, *The Talented Mr. Ripley* opened to strong reviews. What many people didn't realize was that filming the movie was extremely trying for Gwyneth. While she enjoyed her costars and filming in Rome and other locations in Italy, she was unhappy being so far away from her family, especially because both her father and paternal grandfather were seriously ill at the time. She explains: "When I was in Italy shooting Ripley, I got the news that my grandfather, whom I was really close to, had cancer. And then, about six weeks later I got the news that my father had cancer, too."

While Gwyneth's father made it through throat surgery, her grandfather died shortly after seeing his beloved granddaughter win her Oscar. "It changed my life more than anything else," Gwyneth said. "You don't want to get to that place where you're the adult and you're palpably in the next generation. And this shoved my brother and me into that. It was difficult, and sad, and tumultuous."

Few people, other than Minghella, knew about Gwyneth's family worries. "I knew about her concerns, but nobody else on the crew did," he said. "She just tried to keep her head above water throughout it and did it with a great deal of dignity and without a big song and dance about it."

While she struggled offscreen, Gwyneth convincingly became her character onscreen. There was even discussion of Gwyneth getting another Oscar nomination for Best Supporting Actress for her part in *The Talented Mr. Ripley* (although it never came to pass). Costars Matt Damon, who played Ripley, did get an Oscar nomination for Best Actor, while Jude Law, who played Dickie, got one for Best Supporting

Actor. But neither actor walked away with the award.

Seldom resting, Gwyneth had managed to film two more movies—*Duets* and *Bounce*—and star in a successful theater production of *As You Like It* at the Williamstown Theater Festival before *The Talented Mr. Ripley* even premiered. In the spring of 1999, Gwyneth finally got to work with her father on *Duets*, the karaoke comedy he had been planning on filming for years. After Brad Pitt backed out and Bruce Paltrow recovered from throat cancer, Bruce was finally able to work with his daughter.

While Bruce didn't have much of a voice when he first appeared on the set, the director was determined to make the film. Although *Duets* bombed, the father and daughter team relished the experience. Bruce said: "I'd always seen the results of Gwyneth's work, but never

After the success of *The Talented Mr. Ripley*, Gwyneth made two more movies, *Duets* and *Bounce*.

been involved with the process. To be there was just overwhelming. Her instincts are so flawless it's that mind-boggling."

What was even more mind-boggling for some was learning that Gwyneth wasn't only an incredible actress, but she was also a talented singer. Of course, this didn't surprise her family. Danner sang in jazz clubs in college, and Gwyneth's maternal grandfather and uncle were accomplished opera singers. "My mother and I would always sing and harmonize together," Gwyneth recalled. "I was like 3 years old, imitating her jazz-singer way. I was singing that *Sesame Street* song 'One of these things does not belong,' but I put this jazzy spin on it. It was hilarious." In addition to her love of music and her a cappella ensemble at Spence, Gwyneth also remembered Christmases where the whole family would gather around the piano and sing all night long.

Gwyneth sang three songs on the *Duets* soundtrack, "Bette Davis Eyes," "Cruisin'," and "Just My Imagination." The last two were duets performed with Huey Lewis and Babyface, respectively. "Gwyneth is as authentic a talent as you can find, musically speaking," Dick Rudolph, the music supervisor on *Duets* told the press. "The way she phrases stuff, the girl's got it." Some people, including costar Huey Lewis, even told Gwyneth she should make a record, but she declined, saying that she was too busy with her acting.

After Gwyneth finished filming *Duets* in 1999, she went to Williamstown to begin rehearsals for the play *As You Like It.* Gwyneth played Rosalind, who is often called William Shakespeare's most-developed female character, in a stage production that had all of

Hollywood and New York talking. "[I]n disguise as the relentlessly brainy student, she's so convincing that you forget it's Gwyneth Paltrow. But the candid warmth that has made her a star is richly apparent in the epilogue she delivers. She leaves you wanting more," wrote a reviewer for *USA Today*. "Her take on Rosalind has a boldness and broadness, a way of suggesting spontaneity in stylized terms, that could only work in the theater," wrote Ben Brantley of the *New York Times*. "If there is occasionally a curl of affectation in her line readings, you never doubt that Ms. Paltrow knows exactly what she is saying and why she is saying it. It is a thought-through performance that refuses to coast on charm and is poised between delicate moments of insight and comic exaggeration."

The two-week run in August 1999 left Gwyneth with little time to relax: She began filming *Bounce* that fall. Earlier that year, she had managed to convince Affleck to costar in the love story about two people whose lives become entwined after a plane crash.

Gwyneth's character, Abby Janello, is a wife and mother of two whose husband dies in a plane crash just days before Christmas. Affleck plays Buddy Amarall, a successful advertising executive who gave Abby's husband his ticket so he could get back to his family. Guilt-ridden by the crash, Buddy becomes an alcoholic. After he gets help for his addiction, he sets out to find Abby and check on her. What he doesn't bargain for is falling in love with the young widow.

Director and writer Don Roos originally wrote the script with an older couple in mind, but he later rewrote it. Gwyneth agreed to the film first and then Ben came on board. "She wanted to play the part more for Ben than for her," Roos said. "She really thought it was important for Ben to play this part so she kind of made him do it. She said she knew he'd be really wonderful in it. He wanted to do a big action movie, so we owe her a lot."

"It's a movie I'd go see," Gwyneth explained. "I'm not really an explosion-movie type person. I like movies about real people."

Gwyneth's character was a hard-working mother from a middle-class town. Gwyneth dyed her hair brown and wasn't allowed to wear black clothing in the movie (it was considered too stylish). She was forced to do most of her research for the role by going to the grocery store with the children who played her kids. "I don't think she'd ever spent time struggling with those jumbo Tides. But she got it," Roos said. "What you realize is, she's really very ordinary, in the best way, not at all fancy. In this movie, she's like the millions of brave women you find in the supermarket. They have incredible stories of valor in ordinary, day-to-day living. That kind of character really attracts me, and Gwyneth was perfect."

Affleck and Gwyneth were perfect together, too. The chemistry between the two was evident and prompted even more rumors that they were a pair again. The press went so far as to give them one name combining both of theirs— "Benneth." "I don't understand people's fascination," Gwyneth admitted. "If we're in the same city, we go out. We're close. Sometimes when I'm in L.A., I stay in his house. But it's not what people think it is."

Still, Gwyneth has learned that she can be happy with or without a boyfriend in her life.

Despite her busy work schedule, Gwyneth manages to devote time to other projects, especially charities focusing on the environment.

She has plenty else to keep her busy. When she isn't working, she attends yoga classes six times a week; plays with her black Labrador retriever, Holden; spends time with her family and friends; and donates her time to charities, especially those concerned with the environment. Gwyneth said: "I admit to not being a workaholic. I'm much more concerned with leading an interesting life and doing good work. I don't aspire to greatness, and I don't have grandiose ambitions when it comes to acting. Actually, I don't have any killer instinct at all."

Despite saying she isn't ambitious, Gwyneth

has a full schedule planned for the future. She returned to England in late 2000 to film *Possession* and has signed on to star in the Farrelley brothers' comedy *Shallow Hal*, in which she'll play the girl Hal falls in love with—who looks like Gwyneth to him but not to the outside world.

While she relishes her career, Gwyneth has declared that she will not always be in the spotlight. She wants to "take some time off and do normal things. Be a volunteer. . . . Read poetry. Or have a family. . . . But I probably won't have to worry about it. They'll probably kick me out of movies before I'm ready to go." Her many fans will make sure this never happens.

CHRONOLOGY

1972   Born Gwyneth Kate Paltrow on September 28 in Los
        Angeles, California

1983   Paltrow family moves to New York City

1990   Graduates from the Spence School

1991   Enrolls at University of California at Santa Barbara and
        attends classes for one semester; performs in *Picnic* at the
        Williamstown Theater Festival; lands role in Steven
        Spielberg film *Hook; Shout* is released

1993   *Flesh and Bone* and *Malice* are released

1994   *Mrs. Parker and the Vicious Circle* is released

1995   Stars in *Jefferson in Paris, Moonlight and Valentino*, and
        Seven; begins dating Brad Pitt

1996   Stars in *Emma* and *The Pallbearer*; becomes engaged to
        Brad Pitt

1997   Stars in the little-seen *Hard Eight*; ends relationship with
        Pitt; begins dating Ben Affleck

1998   Stars in *Great Expectations, Hush, A Perfect Murder,
        Shakespeare in Love*, and *Sliding Doors*; breaks up
        with Affleck

1999   Wins Screen Actors Guild Award, Golden Globe Award, and
        Academy Award for Best Actress for *Shakespeare in Love*;
        returns to the stage at Williamstown Theater Festival's *As
        You Like It; The Talented Mr. Ripley* is released

2000   Stars in *Duets* and *Bounce*; named one of *Premiere*
        magazine's "Power Elite"

ACCOMPLISHMENTS

Films

1991 *Hook*
      Shout

1993 *Malice*
      Flesh and Bone

1994 *Mrs. Parker and the Vicious Circle*

1995 *Jefferson in Paris*
      Moonlight and Valentino
      Seven

1996 *Emma*
      The Pallbearer

1997 *Hard Eight*

1998 *Hush*
      Great Expectations
      A Perfect Murder
      Shakespeare in Love
      Sliding Doors

1999 *The Talented Mr. Ripley*

2000 *Duets*
      Bounce

Television

1992 *Cruel Doubt*

1993 *Deadly Relations*

FURTHER READING

Hochman, David. "Love's Lady Talks." *Entertainment Weekly,*
  8 January 1999.

Milano, Valerie. *Gwyneth Paltrow.* Toronto, Canada: ECW Press, 2000.

Paltrow, Gwyneth. "Castaway." *Marie Claire.* January 1998.

Rubenstein, Hal. "Gwyneth When She Glitters." *InStyle.* January 1999.

Talley, Andre Leon. "Period Drama." *Vogue.* September 1999.

Official website: http://www.dev.celebsites.com/gwynethpaltrow/

INDEX

PHOTO CREDITS:

2: Colin Mason/London Features Int'l
6: Lisa Rose/ Globe Photos
9: Fitzroy Barrett/ Globe Photos
13: Photofest
14: Bill Ross/Corbis
17: Michael Ferguson/ Globe Photos

21: Kelly Johnson/ Globe Photos
24: Lisa Rose/Globe Photos
29: Photofest
32: Joy E. Scheller/ London Features Int'l
36: Photofest
38: Photofest
40: Sonia Moskowitz/ Globe Photos

45: Joy E. Scheller/ London Features Int'l
47: Dave Parker/ Globe Photos
50: Photofest
53: Dave Bennett/Alpha/ Globe Photos
57: Alec Michael/Globe Photos

Cover photo: Robert Hepler/Everett Collection

ABOUT THE AUTHOR

Award-winning author ANNE E. HILL has been writing for kids and teens since she was a teen herself. This is her 10th biography for young adults. She has also written for a popular line of teen fiction and is currently working on a biography of American movie directors. A Phi Beta Kappa and magna cum laude graduate of Franklin and Marshall College, Anne lives in Wayne, Pennsylvania, with her husband George. A longtime fan of Gwyneth Paltrow, her favorite Gwyneth movie is *Emma*.